An Introduction to Jquery and Javascript

A Fast and Simple Way to Start Creating Web Applications

By Daniel Green

Disclaimer

While all attempts have been made to verify the information provided in this book, the author doesn't assume any responsibility for errors, omissions, or contrary interpretations of the subject matter contained within. **The information provided in this book is for educational and entertainment purposes only. The reader is responsible for his or her own actions, and the author does not accept any responsibilities for any liabilities or damages, real or perceived, resulting from the use of this information.**

Contents

Book Description

This book is about jQuery and Javascript for beginners. The first part of the book explores jQuery in depth, starting with an explanation of what it is. The ways in which one can use jQuery are discussed, including the local installation and the CDN based version.

The book will also guide you on how to call jQuery library functions. JQuery basics, including most of the supported data types and functions are also covered, along with Attributes, which are a common feature in jQuery.

After reading this book, you will know how to handle events in jQuery. You will be able to add actions to most of the jQuery user interface components. JQuery Ajax is also explored, and you will understand how to pass data to the server computer for processing, and then return feedback to the user. You will also know how to create some of the user interface components with jQuery.

The next part of this book explores Javascript in depth. You will know how to declare various types of variables in Javascript. The various methods used for decision making in Javascript are also explored in detail. On reading this book, you will know how to create, read, and delete Javascript cookies. Creation of the various types of dialog boxes is also discussed.

The following topics are explored:

- Definition

- Basics of jQuery

- jQuery Selectors

- jQuery attributes

- Event Handling in jQuery

- jQuery Ajax

- Effects in jQuery

- DOM traversal in jQuery

- jQuery CSS

- jQuery User Interface

- Javascript

- Decision Making in Javascript

- Cookies in Javascript

- Dialog Boxes

Introduction

Both jQuery and Javascript are widely used to create amazing web applications. Javascript is characterized by the ease with which it can be used. JQuery is simply a Javascript library. The languages exhibit a wide range of features, which programmers can use to create web applications with complex functionalities.

One can use Javascript to create a fully functional web application from scratch. In terms of validation, Javascript is very good for that purpose, so take advantage of that and use it. Adding functionality to the user interface with jQuery is very simple, as it is done using Javascript.

Chapter 1: Definition

jQuery is a small, cross-platform, fast and feature-rich Javascript library designed for the purpose of simplifying the client-side scripting of HTML. Today, it forms the most widely used Javascript library. It is characterized by the simplicity with which event handling, HTML document manipulation and traversal, Ajax, and animation are made by use of the API that supports the majority of the browsers currently in use.

Developers also have the option of creating their own plugins and using them on top of the Javascript library. This makes it easy for the developers to create abstractions. Due to the modular approach to the jQuery library, programmers are able to develop powerful web applications and dynamic web pages.

With jQuery, Javascript and HTML are separated. Event handlers on the Data Object Model (DOM) are added using Javascript rather than doing it using HTML event attributes to call Javascript functions. The library also ensures clarity of code due to its features such as shorthand function names and chainable functions. With Javascript, browser compatibility is a problem. However, with jQuery, this problem is solved, since programmers can create web pages which can run on a variety of browsers. Extension of the framework using jQuery is also very simple.

How it is used

There are two ways that one can use jQuery. These include the following:

- **CDN Based Version** – this method involves including the jQuery library into your HTML code from a Content Delivery Network (CDN).

- **Local Installation** – this method involves downloading jQuery library on your local machine, and then including it in the HTML code.

Local Installation

To install the library locally, you must first download it onto your local machine. Save it in the same directory as your website. After this, you can include it in your HTML code as follows:

```
<html>

<head>

<title>First jQuery example</title>

<script type="text/javascript" src="/jquery/jquery-2.1.3.min.js"></script>

<script type="text/javascript">

$(document).ready(function(){

document.write("Hello, Welcome to jQuery!");});

</script>

</head>
```

```
<body>

<h1>Welcome to jQuery</h1>

</body>

</html>
```

Note that the file containing the above code must be saved with a name containing the ".*html*" extension. You can then open the file using your browser. A window will be displayed with the following text:

Hello, Welcome to jQuery!

The CDN based version is the simplest to use, since you just have to specify the URL where the jQuery is located. This is illustrated with the following example:

```
<html>

<head>
```

```html
<title>The jQuery Example</title>

<script type="text/javascript"
src="http://ajax.googleapis.com/ajax/libs/jquery/2.1.3/j
query.min.js">

</script>
```

```html
<script type="text/javascript">

$(document).ready(function(){

document.write("Hello, Welcome to jQuery!");

});

</script>

</head>

<body>

<h1>Hello World</h1>
```

</body>

</html>

Again, give the file a name with an ".*html*" extension. After this, open it with your favorite browser. The same result as in our first example will be obtained as shown below:

Hello, Welcome to jQuery!

Calling jQuery Library Functions

For an event to work on your web page, then call it inside the function *"$(document).ready()"*. Once the DOM is loaded, and before the contents of the page are loaded, everything inside this function is loaded.

We must begin by registering a ready event for the document as shown below:

```
<html>

<head>

<title>jQuery sample program</title>

<script type="text/javascript"
src="http://ajax.googleapis.com/ajax/libs/jquery/2.1.3/jquery.min.js">

</script>

<script type="text/javascript" language="javascript">

$(document).ready(function() {
```

```
$("div").click(function() {alert("Hello, welcome to
jQuery");});

});

</script>

</head>

<body>

<div id="mdiv">

Click here and a dialogue will appear.

</div>

</body>

</html>
```

Once again, save the file with the above contents with an ".*html*" extension in the name. You can then open it using your favorite browser. A window with the following content will be observed:

Click here and a dialogue will appear.

Click on the text to see the dialogue being talked about. The dialog will appear as follows:

Chapter 2:

Basics of jQuery

In this chapter, we will tackle the most frequently used concepts in jQuery.

Numbers

In jQuery, numbers are immutable, and they take double precision 64-bit format IEEE 754 values. The examples shown below are valid number in jQuery:

6780

230.42

0.47

<u>String</u>

It is an immutable character in Javascript that takes one, many, or even no characters. The following are examples of strings in Javascript:

"An example of a Javascript string"

'Javascript is easy to learn'

'A good "String" in Javascript'

"An 'example' of a JavaScript String"

<u>Boolean</u>

The value of a Boolean operator can either be a *"true"* or a *"false."* Zero and empty will always default to false.

Arrays

Arrays are used for storing values or objects. They are defined as follows:

var i = [];

var j = [5,6,7,8,9];

For the purpose of performing an iteration, arrays have values as illustrated in the example below:

var i = [1, 2, 3, 4, 5];

for (var j = 0; i < i.length; j++) {

// perform an action with x[i]

}

Objects

It is possible to use objects in Javascript. We use the object to create objects in Javascript. This is shown below:

```
var n = {

name: "Mike",

age: 35

};
```

To read or write the properties of an object, the dot notation is used. This is demonstrated using the following example:

```
// Get the properties of the object

n.name  // ==> Mike

n.age   // ==> 35



// Set the properties of the object
```

n.name = "John" // <== John

n.age = 30 // <== 30

Functions

In Javascript, functions can be either anonymous or named. To create a named function, we use the *"function"* keyword. This is shown below:

function namedfunction(){

// add your content here

}

To define an anonymous function, do this in the normal way, but do not include a function name. Just pass it to a method or assign it to a variable as shown in the example below:

var h = function (){

// add your content here

}

To make use of an anonymous function, jQuery does as follows:

```
$(document).ready(function(){

// add your content here

});
```

Arguments

This is a special kind of array with a *"length"* property. Consider the example shown below:

```
function f(y){

console.log(typeof y, arguments.length);

}

f();          //==> "undefined", 0
```

f(1);   //==> "number", 1

f("1", "2", "3");   //==> "string", 3

A *"callee"* property for the object of the argument is also present as shown below:

function f() {

return arguments.callee;

}

f();   // ==> f

Scope

This defines the region where a variable is declared. There are only two variable scopes in Javascript:

- **Global Variables** – this is a variable defined everywhere in Javascript, meaning that its scope is global.

- **Local Variables** –this is a variable which is only available or visible within the function of a declaration. The parameters of a function are visible only to that function.

Within a function's body, a local variable will take precedence over a global variable having a similar name. Consider the example shown below:

var mVariable = "global";   // ==> declaring a global variable

function ( ) {

var mVariable = "local"; // ==> declaring a local variable

document.write(mVariable); // ==> local

}

Chapter 3:

jQuery Selectors

With jQuery selectors, we can easily and quickly access groups of elements in the Data Object Model (DOM). They are used to search for certain expressions depending on the criteria that we specify. The selected items can then be used for us to perform various operations.

"$() factory" function

In jQuery, selectors begin with a dollar sign, and the parenthesis, that is, "$()". To select elements from a DOM object, the factory function makes use of the following building blocks:

- **Tag Name** – used to represent a tag name present in the DOM. Example, **$('ph')** will select all paragraphs <ph> in the document.

- **Tag Class** –used to represent a tag present with the given class in the DOM. Example, **$('.a-class')** will select all the elements contained in the document having a class of "*a-class*".

- **Tag ID** –used to represent a tag available with the given ID in the DOM. Example, **$('#an-id')** will select a single element in the document having an ID of "*an-id*".

Consider the example shown below:

<html>

<head>

```html
<title>jQuery sample program</title>

<script type="text/javascript"
src="http://ajax.googleapis.com/ajax/libs/jquery/2.1.3/jquery.min.js">

</script>

<script type="text/javascript"
language="javascript">

$(document).ready(function() {

$("ph").css("background-color", "yellow");

});

</script>

</head>

<body>
```

```
<div>

<p class="jclass">An example of a paragraph.</p>

<p id="mid">A second paragraph example.</p>

<p>A third paragraph example.</p>

</div>

</body>

</html>
```

You can write the above program, and then open it with your favorite browser. The following output will be observed:

An example of a paragraph.

A second paragraph example.

A third paragraph example.

All elements whose tag name is "*p*" have been selected, and their background has been set to a "*yellow*" color.

Chapter 4:

jQuery Attributes

Attributes and the properties of a DOM element can easily be manipulated. To fetch the value of an attribute in jQuery, we use the method "*attr()*". The attribute is always fetched from the first element in the matched set. Consider the example program given below:

```
<html>

<head>

<title>A jQuery program</title>

<script type="text/javascript"
src="http://ajax.googleapis.com/ajax/libs/jquery/2.1.
3/jquery.min.js">
```

```
</script>

<script type="text/javascript"
language="javascript">

$(document).ready(function() {

var t = $("em").attr("t");

$("#div").text(t);

});

</script>

</head>


<body>

<div>
```

```html
<em title="Bold and Brave">An example of a
paragraph.</em>

<p id="myid">A second example of a paragraph.</p>

<div id="div"></div>

</div>

</body>

</html>
```

You can then save the program. Give the file a name with an ".html" extension, otherwise, you will get errors. You can then run it by opening it using your favorite browser. You will observe the following output:

An example of a paragraph.

A second example of a paragraph.

Setting the value of an Attribute

You might need to set a named attribute onto all the elements in the wrapped set. This is usually done using the passed value and the method "**attr(name, value)**" is used. Consider the example shown below:

```
<html>

<head>

<title>jQuery sample program</title>

<script type="text/javascript"
src="http://ajax.googleapis.com/ajax/libs/jquery/2.1.
3/jquery.min.js">

</script>

<script type="text/javascript"
language="javascript">
```

```
$(document).ready(function() {

$("#myimg").attr("src", "/images/image.jpg");

});

</script>

</head>

<body>

<div>

<img id="img" src="img.jpg" alt="An image" />

</div>

</body>

</html>
```

You can set the path of the image to where you have stored your image. This also applies to the name of the image. The program will set the attribute *"src"* of the image tag to the correct location. After running the program, the output will be the image alongside the text that we specified. Consider the example given below:

```
<html>

<head>

<title>jQuery sample program</title>

<script type="text/javascript"
src="http://ajax.googleapis.com/ajax/libs/jquery/2.1.
3/jquery.min.js">

</script>
```

```
<script type="text/javascript"
language="javascript">

$(document).ready(function() {

$("em").addClass("selected");

$("#mid").addClass("highlight");

});

</script>

<style>

.selected { color:red; }

.highlight { background:yellow; }

</style>

</head>

<body>
```

```
<em title="Bold and Brave">A paragraph example
with jQuery.</em>

<p id="mid">A second paragraph example.</p>

</body>

</html>
```

You can save the file, and then open it with the browser. You
will get the following output:

A paragraph example with jQuery.

A second paragraph example.

Chapter 5:
Event Handling in jQuery

With events, we can create dynamic web pages. They are simply actions which the web applications that we create can detect. The following are some of the available events in jQuery:

- Keyboard keystroke event

- mouse click event

- mouse over event

- web page loading event

- Submission of an HTML form event

What happens is that after the event is detected, you can specify what is to happen or what is to be done via coding.

Event Handlers Binging

To do this, we use the *"bind()"* method. Consider the example program given below:

<html>

<head>

<title>A jQuery sample program</title>

<script type="text/javascript"
src="http://ajax.googleapis.com/ajax/libs/jquery/2.1.
3/jquery.min.js"></script>

<script type="text/javascript"
language="javascript">

$(document).ready(function() {

```
$('div').bind('click', function( event ){

alert('Hello');

});

});

</script>

<style>

.div{ margin:10px;padding:12px; border:2px solid
#666; width:60px;}

</style>

</head>

<body>

<p>Choose a square and click on it to see what
happens:</p>
```

```html
<div class="div" style="background-color:green;">Click 1</div>

<div class="div" style="background-color:yellow;">Click 2</div>

<div class="div" style="background-color:blue;">Click 3</div>

</body>

</html>
```

Write the program above. Once done, just save it with a suitable name. Don't forget to include the "*.html*" extension in the file name. After saving, open it with a favorite browser. The following output will be observed:

Choose a square and click on it to see what happens:

The above figure shows the output, which is made up of three

buttons, each with a different color. Click on the first button,

and observe what happens. The following dialog will appear:

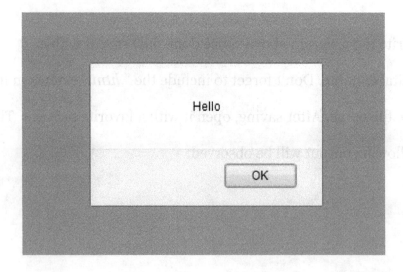

The text on the dialog is the one that we specified in our program. Now exit the dialog, and then click on the second button. The same dialog will appear again. Click on the final button, and observe what happens. The same dialog will appear. This is a good example of how events work in Javascript. What we have done is that we handled a click event on the three buttons, so after clicking, the dialog appears. You can specify something else to happen after clicking on the button other than triggering the dialog.

Consider the following example:

<html>

<head>

<title>A jQuery sample program</title>

```
<script type="text/javascript"
src="http://ajax.googleapis.com/ajax/libs/jquery/2.1.
3/jquery.min.js"></script>

<script type="text/javascript"
language="javascript">

$(document).ready(function() {

$('div').bind('click', function( e ){

alert('The event is of type ' + e.type);

alert('pageX : ' + e.pageX);

alert('pageY : ' + e.pageY);

alert('The target is : ' + e.target.innerHTML);

});

});
```

```
</script>

<style>

.div{ margin:10px;padding:12px; border:2px solid
#666; width:60px;}

</style>

</head>

<body>

<p>Choose a square and click on it to see what
happens:</p>

<div class="div" style="background-
color:green;">Click 1</div>

<div class="div" style="background-
color:yellow;">Click 2</div>
```

```
<div class="div" style="background-color:blue;">Click 3</div>

</body>

</html>
```

Save the file, and then open it with a browser. You will get the following window as the result:

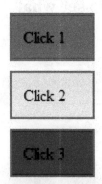

Although the window is the same as the one that we created in our previous example, the difference comes in when it comes to handling the events. Just click on the first button. The following dialog will appear:

You can then click on the second and the third button, and you will get the same dialog box. This is another way that we can handle events with jQuery. This method has also introduced new properties available in jQuery for accessing objects.

Chapter 6:
jQuery Ajax

Ajax stands for Asynchronous Javascript and XML. With it, we can load data from the server without having to refresh the web page. With jQuery, you can make use of a variety of Ajax methods to develop modern applications.

To load data with Ajax in jQuery, we use the *"load()"* method. This takes the following syntax:

[selector].load(URL, [data], [callback]);

The following is an explanation of the parameters in the above syntax:

- **URL** – this is the URL of the resource on the server side to which a request will be sent. This can be a CGI, JSP, ASP, or PHP script which generates data from a database or dynamically.

- **data** – This is an optional parameter. It is used to represent the object whose properties are to be serialized into the properly encoded parameters aimed for passing to the request. If this is specified, the "POST" method is used to send the request. If not specified, then we use the "GET" method.

- **callback** – this function is invoked after loading the response data into the elements of the matched set. The response text received from the server forms the first parameter passed to this function. The second parameter is the status code.

Consider the following jQuery program:

```html
<html>

<head>

<title>A jQuery sample program</title>

<script type="text/javascript"
src="http://ajax.googleapis.com/ajax/libs/jquery/2.1.
3/jquery.min.js"></script> <script
type="text/javascript" language="javascript">

$(document).ready(function() {

$("#d").click(function(e){

$('#s').load('/jquery/r.html');

});

});

</script>
```

```
</head>

<body>

<p>Click here to load the file: /jquery/r.html  -</p>

<div id="s" style="background-color:cc0;">

Click on the Button below

</div>

<input type="button" id="d" value="Load" />

</body>

</html>
```

You can then save the file with a suitable name. Open it with a browser. A window will appear with a button written "*Load*". Click on the button, and observe what will happen. If you have specified the right file, the one available on your local machine, then it will be loaded. The path to the file should also be correct.

Passing the data to server

Once data has been collected from the user, there is a need to pass it to the server for the purpose of processing. With jQuery Ajax, this can be done with a lot of ease. The data parameter of the available Ajax method can be used.

In the next example, we are going to demonstrate how user input is sent to the server, the server processes it, and then sends back the result. We finally print the result.

The following is the example:

<html>

<head>

<title>A jQuery sample program</title>

```
<script type="text/javascript"
src="http://ajax.googleapis.com/ajax/libs/jquery/2.1.
3/jquery.min.js"></script>

<script type="text/javascript"
language="javascript">

$(document).ready(function() {

$("#d").click(function(e){

var n = $("#n").val();

$("#s").load('/jquery/r.php', {"n":n} );

});

});

</script>

</head>
```

```html
<body>

<p>First provide your name and then click the button:</p>

<input type="input" id="name" size="40" /><br />

<div id="s" style="background-color:cc0;">

Look here!

</div>

<input type="button" id="d" value="Click" />

</body>

</html>
```

You can then run the file after saving it. A window will appear prompting you to enter your name. This is shown in the figure below:

First provide your name and then click the button:

Look here!

Click

Just do so in the provided text field. Click on the button written "*Click,*" and observe what will happen. This is illustrated in the figure shown below:

Mike

Welcome Mike

In the above figure, it is clear that after entering the name and clicking on the button, I get a welcome message with the name I just provided. The name has been sent to the server, the server has processed the name, and then it has sent the results back. We have then printed the results to the user.

Chapter 7:
Effects in jQuery

With jQuery, one can add amazing effects to their applications for user attraction and satisfaction.

Hiding and showing elements

To do this, we simply use the *"hide()"* method for hiding elements, and the *"show()"* method for showing elements. The *"hide()"* method takes the following syntax:

[selector].hide(speed, [callback]);

The following parameters have been used:

- **speed** – this is a string used to represent one of the three predefined speeds, that is, slow, normal, or fast. This can also be the number of seconds for which an animation will be run.

- **callback** – this parameter is optional, and is used to represent the function to be executed at any time the animation completes for each element which has been animated against it, it will execute only once.

The "*show()*" method takes the following syntax:

[selector].show(speed, [callback]);

The following parameters have been used:

- **speed** – this is a string used to represent one of the three predefined speeds, that is, slow, normal ,or fast. This can also be the number of seconds for which an animation will be run.

- **callback** – this parameter is optional and is used to represent the function to be executed at any time the animation completes for each element which has been animated against it, it will execute only once.

Consider the example given below:

```
<html>

<head>

<title>A jQuery sample program</title>

<script type="text/javascript"
src="http://ajax.googleapis.com/ajax/libs/jquery/2.1.
3/jquery.min.js"></script>

<script type="text/javascript"
language="javascript">

$(document).ready(function() {

$("#s").click(function () {
```

```
$(".mdiv").show( 900 );

});

$("#h").click(function () {

$(".mdiv").hide( 900 );

});

});

</script>

<style>

.mdiv{ margin:10px;padding:12px; border:2px solid
#666; width:100px; height:100px;}

</style>

</head>

<body>
```

```
<div class="mdiv">

A sample Square

</div>

<input id="h" type="button" value="Hide" />

<input id="s" type="button" value="Show" />

</body>

</html>
```

You can write the program, and then save it with a ".*html*"
extension in the name. Open it with your browser. The
following output will be observed:

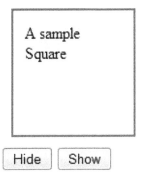

Click on the "*hide*" button, and observe what will happen. The square will disappear and you will be left with the following:

Now, click on the "*show*" button and observe the effect. The square will reappear, and you will be back to normal. This is a good demonstration of the hide and show effect in jQuery.

Toggle effect

With jQuery, one can toggle how an element is displayed, between states of either hidden or revealed. If the element is already shown, then it will become hidden, and if hidden, then it will definitely be shown. To do this, we simply use the *"toggle()"* method which takes the following syntax:

[selector]..toggle([speed][, callback]);

The following parameters have been used in the above syntax:

- **speed** – this is a string used to represent one of the three predefined speeds, that is, slow, normal, or fast. This can also be the number of seconds for which an animation will be run.

- **callback** – this parameter is optional, and is used to represent the function to be executed at any time the animation completes for each element which has been animated against it, it will execute only once.

Let us demonstrate this with an example:

\<html\>

\<head\>

\<title\>A jQuery sample program\</title\>

\<script type="text/javascript" src="http://ajax.googleapis.com/ajax/libs/jquery/2.1.3/jquery.min.js"\>\</script\>

\<script type="text/javascript" language="javascript"\>

$(document).ready(function() {

```
$(".click").click(function(e){

$(".target").toggle('slow', function(){

$(".log").text('A complete transition);

});

});

});

</script>

<style>

.click{ margin:10px;padding:12px; border:2px solid
#666; width:100px; height:50px;}

</style>

</head>

<body>
```

```html
<div class="content">

<div class="click">Click Here</div>

<div class="target">

<img src="./ img.jpg" alt="image" />

</div>

<div class="log"></div>

</div>

</body>

</html>
```

You can then save the program, and open the file with a browser. You will observe the following output:

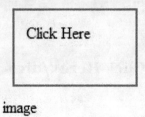

image

Just click the image, and observe what will happen. The text written *"image"* will disappear and the one written" *A complete transition"* will occur.

The above are examples of some of the effects available in jQuery. However, there are many other effects, so you can learn them on your own.

Chapter 8:

DOM traversal in jQuery

With jQuery, we can traverse the DOM elements, and then select the elements in our document either sequentially or randomly. In most cases, most of the traversal methods in use do not have a modification effect on the document, but they just filter some parts based on the criteria being specified. Consider the example given below:

\<html\>

\<head\>

\<title\>A JQuery sample program\</title\>

\</head\>

\<body\>

```
<div>

<ul>

<li>first item</li>

<li>second item</li>

<li>third item</li>

<li>fourth item</li>

<li>fifth item</li>

<li>sixth item</li>

<li>seventh item</li>

</ul>

</div>

</body>
```

</html>

Just write the program, save the file, and then open it with your browser. You will observe the following output:

- first item
- second item
- third item
- fourth item
- fifth item
- sixth item
- seventh item

In the above example, every item has its own index. This means that locating any of the items can be done easily. It is worth noting that indices start at zero, meaning that "*second item*" is at index 1. Consider the example given below:

<html>

```html
<head>

<title>A sample jQuery program</title>

<script type="text/javascript"
src="http://ajax.googleapis.com/ajax/libs/jquery/2.1.3/jquery.min.js">

</script>

<script type="text/javascript"
language="javascript">

$(document).ready(function() {

$("li").eq(3).addClass("selected");

});

</script>

<style>
```

```
.selected { color:blue; }

</style>

</head>

<body>

<div>

<ul>

<li>first item</li>

<li>second item</li>

<li>third item</li>

<li>fourth item</li>

<li>fifth item</li>

<li>sixth item</li>
```

```html
<li>seventh item</li>

</ul>

</div>

</body>

</html>
```

The above program will give the following output:

- first item
- second item
- third item
- fourth item
- fifth item
- sixth item
- seventh item

The item at index 3, which is the *"fourth item,"* has been selected, and its color has been changed to blue. This is a good example about how to select elements using indices in jQuery.

Filtering elements

To filter out some elements which do not match the specified criteria, we use the *"filter(selector)"* method. There are numerous selector syntax and one is free to use any one suitable for their purpose. Consider the example program shown below:

<html>

<head>

<title>A sample jQuery program</title>

<script type="text/javascript"
src="http://ajax.googleapis.com/ajax/libs/jquery/2.1.
3/jquery.min.js">

```html
</script>

<script type="text/javascript"
language="javascript">

$(document).ready(function() {

$("li").filter(".middle").addClass("selected");

});

</script>

<style>

.selected { color:blue; }

</style>

</head>

<body>

<div>
```

```html
<ul>

<li class="top">first item</li>

    <li class="top">second item</li>

    <li class="middle">third item</li>

    <li class="middle">fourth item</li>

    <li class="bottom">fifth item</li>

  <li class="bottom">sixth item</li> </ul>

</div>

</body>

</html>
```

Just run the program after saving it. You will observe the

following output:

- first item
- second item
- third item
- fourth item
- fifth item
- sixth item

You notice that all lists associated with the "*middle*" class have been selected, and their color changed to blue.

Location of Descendent Elements

To do this, we can use the "*find (selector)*" method. The selector also has numerous syntax, so one is free to use the right one for their app. Consider the following example:

```
<html>

<head>

<title>A sample jQuery program</title>

<script type="text/javascript"
src="http://ajax.googleapis.com/ajax/libs/jquery/2.1.
3/jquery.min.js">

</script>

<script type="text/javascript"
language="javascript">

$(document).ready(function() {
```

```
$("p").find("span").addClass("selected");

});

</script>

<style>

.selected { color:blue; }

</style>

</head>

<body>

<p>This forms the first paragraph and<span>It is
Blue</span></p>

<p> This forms the second paragraph and <span>It is
also Blue</span></p>

</body>
```

</html>

You can save the program, and then open the file with your

browser. You will observe the following output:

This forms the first paragraph andIt is Blue

This forms the second paragraph and It is also Blue

As observed, elements within the "*<span>*" tag are selected,

and their color has been changed to blue.

Chapter 9:
jQuery CSS

Withthe jQuery library, developers can enhance the look of their websites by making use of the selector methods in a CSS (Cascading Style Sheet). To apply a CSS property in jQuery, use the method *"css(PropertyName, PropertyValue)",* which takes the following syntax:

selector.css(PropertyName, PropertyValue);

Consider the example shown below:

<html>

  <head>

    <title>A jQuery sample program</title>

```html
<script type="text/javascript"
src="http://ajax.googleapis.com/ajax/libs/jquery/2.1.
3/jquery.min.js"></script>

    <script type="text/javascript"
language="javascript">

  $(document).ready(function() {

    $("div:first").width(110);

    $("div:first").css("background-color", "red");

  });

</script>


<style>

  div{ width:70px; height:50px; float:left;
margin:5px; background:yellow; cursor:pointer; }
```

```html
    </style>


</head>

        <body>

    <div>i</div>

    <div>h</div>

    <div>h</div>

    <div>h</div>

</body>

        </html>
```

After saving the program, open the file with a browser, and you will observe the following output:

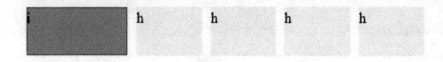

The example shows how we can use CSS in our web app using jQuery.

Chapter 10:
jQuery User Interface

The JQuery User Interface (UI) is made up of widgets, themes, effects, and a set of user interface interactions, which are available in the jQuery Javascript library. If you need to develop a web application which is highly interactive, then use jQuery, as it is the best choice for that.

Let us examine how to create some of the widgets available in jQuery:

Button

It is possible to create buttons in jQuery. Let us demonstrate using an example.

Write the program shown below:

```html
<!doctype html>

<html lang="en">

<head>

<meta charset="utf-8">

<title>A Button in jQuery</title>

<link rel="stylesheet"
href="//code.jquery.com/ui/1.11.4/themes/smoothne
ss/jquery-ui.css">

<script src="//code.jquery.com/jquery-
1.10.2.js"></script>

<script src="//code.jquery.com/ui/1.11.4/jquery-
ui.js"></script>
```

```
<link rel="stylesheet"
href="/resources/demos/style.css">

<script>

$(function() {

$( "input[type=submit], a, button" )

.button()

.click(function( event ) {

event.preventDefault();

});

});

</script>

</head>

<body>
```

```
<button>The button</button>

<input type="submit" value="submit button">

<a href="#">Anchor</a>

</body>

</html>
```

You can save the program. Open it with your browser, and observe the result. The following will be the output:

The button   submit button   Anchor

The example clearly shows how creating a button in jQuery is simple.

Autocomplete

With the autocomplete, you are provided with options as you type in the text box. These options are usually specified in your code. Consider the example shown below:

```
<!doctype html>

<html lang="en">

<head>

<meta charset="utf-8">

<title>A sample jQuery autocomplete view</title>

<link rel="stylesheet"
href="//code.jquery.com/ui/1.11.4/themes/smoothne
ss/jquery-ui.css">
```

```html
<script src="//code.jquery.com/jquery-
1.10.2.js"></script>

<script src="//code.jquery.com/ui/1.11.4/jquery-
ui.js"></script>

<link rel="stylesheet"
href="/resources/demos/style.css">

<script>

$(function() {

var presentOptions = [

"Apple",

"Atom",

"Angela",

"Boy",
```

"Cut",

"Cat",

"Closure",

"COBOL",

"Command",

"England",

"Fortran",

"Google",

"Hatchet",

"Java",

"Jumbo",

"Lisp",

```
"Pascal",

"Photo",

"Python",

"Rails",

"Social",

"Scheme"

];

$( "#tags" ).autocomplete({

source: presentOptions

});

});

</script>
```

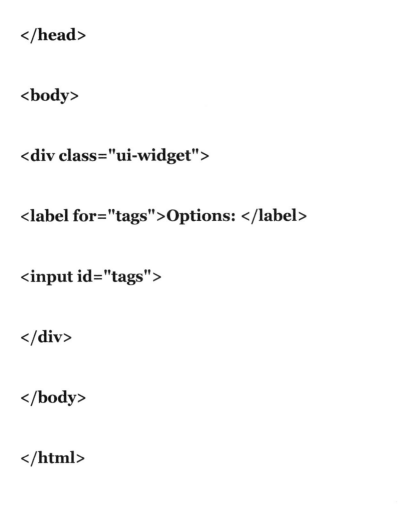

```
</head>

<body>

<div class="ui-widget">

<label for="tags">Options: </label>

<input id="tags">

</div>

</body>

</html>
```

You can then save the program, and then open it with your browser. You will observe the following output:

Options: [   ]

You can then try to type any of the options which we have specified. They will be suggested. You have the choice of selecting the right suggestion for yourself.

Chapter 11:
Javascript

It is the most widely used programming language in the world. It is an object-oriented programming language and with it, programmers can develop interactive web pages. The language is interpreted, rather than being compiled.

Variable Declaration in Javascript

To declare variables in Javascript, we use the keyword "*var*". This is shown below:

```
<script type="text/javascript">

<!--
```

```
var fruit;

var name;

//-->

</script>
```

A single *"var"* keyword can be used to declare multiple variables at once. This is demonstrated below:

```
<script type="text/javascript">

<!--

var fruit, name;

//-->

</script>
```

It is also possible to initialize variables at their time of declaration. This is demonstrated below:

```
<script type="text/javascript">

<!--

var fruit = "Mango";

var weight;

weight = 2.6;

//-->

</script>
```

Notice that in the above example, we have declared the variables and then assigned values to them. This is called *"initialization."*

Chapter 12:

Decision Making in Javascript

While programming, you might reach a point where decision making should be applied. Let us discuss some of the decision making statements in Javascript.

The "if" statement

This allows Javascript to execute statements once a certain condition has been met. It takes the following syntax:

if (consition){

Statement(s) to be executed once the condition is met

}

With the above syntax, once the condition is met, then the statement(s) will then be executed. If not met, then no statement(s) will be executed. In most cases, comparison operators are used in decision making. Consider the following example:

```
<script type="text/javascript">

<!--

var position = 10;

if( position <20 ){

document.write("<b>You are qualified to proceed to the next class</b>");

}

//-->

</script>
```

Once again, save the program with the file name having an ".html" extension. Open it with your browser, and you will get the following output:

You are qualified to proceed to the next class

The "if...else" statement

With this condition, one can make several decisions if more conditions are to be involved. This means that it is an advanced form of making decisions in Javascript. It takes the following syntax:

if (condition 1){

Statement(s) to be executed if the condition 1 is met

}else if (condition 2){

Statement(s) to be executed if the condition 2 is met

}else if (consition 3){

Statement(s) to be executed if the condition 3 is met

}else{

Statement(s) to be executed if no condition is met

}

The syntax is easy to understand, as the statement(s) will be executed if and only if their condition is met. Consider the following example:

```
<script type="text/javascript">

<!--

var grade = "B";

if( grade == "A" ){

document.write("<b>That's excellent</b>");

}else if( grade == "B" ){

document.write("<b>That's good</b>");
```

```
}else if( book == "C" ){

document.write("<b>That's fair</b>");

}else{

document.write("<b>You have failed or unknown
grade</b>");

}

//-->

</script>
```

Again, save the file, and then open it with your browser. You will get the following result:

That's good

This is the value of the grade that has been initialized to "**B.**" You can try to change the value of the grade and then observe how the output changes.

Switch Case

The above statements are not always the best for use. What if the branches on a single variable value? This calls for the use of the "*case*" statement. It takes the following syntax:

switch (expression)

{

case 1st condition : statement(s)

break;

case 2nd condition: statement(s)

break;

...

case nth condition: statement(s)

break;

default: statement(s)

}

When the interpreter meets the "break" statement, it will know that the case has ended. If you fail to include this, then the interpreter will work on all the case statements. Consider the following example:

<script type="text/javascript">

<!--

var grade='B';

**document.write("Beginning to process the switch statement
");**

```
switch (grade)

{

case 'A': document.write("That's excellent<br />");

break;

case 'B': document.write("That's good <br />");

break;

case 'C': document.write("That's fair <br />");

break;

case 'D': document.write("That's a pass <br />");

break;

case 'F': document.write("You terribly failed<br />");

break;
```

default: document.write("The grade is not available

**
")**

}

document.write("Just about to exit the switch

block");

//-->

</script>

You can save the program, and then run it. The following

output will be observed:


```
Beginning to process the switch statement
That's good
Just about to exit the switch block
```

The above figure shows the output from the program. Note that we have initialized the value of grade to "*B,*" and this explains the source of the "*That's good*" statement in the output.

To demonstrate the importance of "*break*" in the program, run the following program:

```
<script type="text/javascript">

<!--

var grade='B';

document.write("Beginning to process the switch statement<br />");

switch (grade)

{
```

```
case 'A': document.write("That's excellent<br />");

case 'B': document.write("That's good <br />");

case 'C': document.write("That's fair <br />");

case 'D': document.write("That's a pass <br />");

case 'F': document.write("You terribly failed<br />");

default:  document.write("The grade is not available
<br />")

}

document.write("Just about to exit the switch
block");

//-->

</script>
```

The program will give the following output:

Beginning to process the switch statement
That's good
That's fair
That's a pass
You terribly failed
The grade is not available
Just about to exit the switch block

This shows that without the *"break"* statement, the interpreter interprets all the case conditions at once, since it does not know the end of any case statement.

"While" Loop

This forms the widely used loop in Javascript. It has the following syntax:

while (condition){

Statement(s) to be executed if the condition is met.

}

The loop operates in that as long as the specified condition is true, then the loop is executed. Execution stops only when the condition becomes false. Consider the example shown below:

<script type="text/javascript">

<!--

```javascript
var c = 0;

document.write("The loop is starting" + "<br />");

while (c < 5){

document.write("Current value of c : " + c + "<br
/>");

c++;

}

document.write("The loop has stopped execution!");

//-->

</script>
```

You can write the above program, and then save it. Open it
with your browser, and observe the output. The following will
be the result:

```
The loop is starting
Current value of c : 0
Current value of c : 1
Current value of c : 2
Current value of c : 3
Current value of c : 4
The loop has stopped execution!
```

Notice that the value of variable "c" is incremented until it reaches the value of 4. This is because we specified it to be less than 5. When the interpreter finds that the value of the variable is more than 4, then it stops execution.

The "do…while" Loop

In this loop, the condition check takes place at the end of the loop. This interprets to the fact that even if the condition is false, the loop must be executed at least once. It has the following syntax:

do{

Statement(s) for execution;

} while (expression);

A semicolon must be used at the end of the check condition. Consider the following example:

<script type="text/javascript">

<!--

```javascript
var c = 0;

document.write("The loop is being started" + "<br />");

do{

document.write("The current value of variable c : " +
c + "<br />");

c++;

}while (c < 5);

document.write("The loop has stopped!");

//-->

</script>
```

You can write the program, save it, and then open it with your browser. Do not forget the ".*html*" extension in the name. The output of the above program should be as follows:

The loop is being started
The current value of variable c : 0
The current value of variable c : 1
The current value of variable c : 2
The current value of variable c : 3
The current value of variable c : 4
The loop has stopped!

Suppose that we set the value of the variable "*c*" to be less than 0, what will happen? Let us demonstrate this using the following example:

<script type="text/javascript">

<!--

var c = 0;

```javascript
document.write("The loop is being started" + "<br />");

do{

document.write("The current value of variable c : " + c + "<br />");

c++;

}while (c < 0);

document.write("The loop has stopped!");

//-->

</script>
```

Again, you can write the program, save it, and then open the file using your browser. The program should give the following output:

The loop is being started
The current value of variable c : 0
The loop has stopped!

Although we have set the value of the variable to be less than

0, it still executes, but only once. Remember what we said, that

the loop must be executed at least once even if the condition

has not been set. This is what has happened in our case.

The "for" loop

This loop involves initializing the initial value of the variable, test condition, and the iteration itself. It has the following syntax:

for (initial value; testing condition; iteration statement){

Statement(s) to be executed when the test condition is met

}

Consider the example given below:

<script type="text/javascript">

<!--

```javascript
var c;

document.write("The loop is starting" + "<br />");

for(c = 0; c < 5; c++){

  document.write("The current value of c : " + c );

  document.write("<br />");

}

document.write("The loop has stopped!");

//-->

</script>
```

Write the program, save it, and then open it in your browser.
You should get the following output:

```
The loop is starting
The current value of c : 0
The current value of c : 1
The current value of c : 2
The current value of c : 3
The current value of c : 4
The loop has stopped!
```

Again, five is not included in the output, as the value of the variable is set to less than that. The loop will stop execution when it finds itself violating the condition.

The "for…in" Loop

This is used to loop through the properties of an object. It takes the following syntax:

for (nameofvarible in object){

block or statement to be executed

}

After a single iteration, one of the object's properties is assigned to a variable. The iteration continues until each of the properties of the object is assigned to a variable. Consider the following example:

<script type="text/javascript">

<!--

```javascript
var objectProperty;

document.write("Navigating the properties of the object<br /> ");

for (objectProperty in navigator)

{

document.write(objectProperty);

document.write("<br />");

}

document.write("Now leaving the loop!");

//-->

</script>
```

You can write the program and then save it. Open it with your browser and observe the output. The result should be the Navigator object of your web browser. On my system, it gives the following result:

```
Navigating the properties of the object
mozPay
mozContacts
mozApps
mozTCPSocket
vibrate
javaEnabled
getGamepads
mozGetUserMedia
sendBeacon
registerProtocolHandler
registerContentHandler
taintEnabled
mimeTypes
```

This is not the end as the list continues.

Controlling the Loop in Javascript

With Javascript, you can exercise full control of your loop and the switch statement. At certain times, you might need to skip execution of certain parts of the loop or not execute some parts of the loop at all. To achieve this, one can make use of the "*break*" and the "*continue*" statements which are available in Javascript.

The "break" statement

The statement is only used when one wants to leave the loop early and exit the curly braces. Let us illustrate how this statement can be used with the "*while*" statement:

```
<script type="text/javascript">

<!--
```

```javascript
var y = 0;

document.write("Getting into the loop<br /> ");

while (y < 10)

{

if (y == 5){

break;  // this will completely break out of the loop

}

y = y + 1;

document.write( y + "<br />");

}

document.write("Now leaving the loop!<br /> ");

//-->
```

</script>

You can save the program, and then open it with your browser.

You will observe the following output:

Getting into the loop
1
2
3
4
5
Now leaving the loop!

What has happened is that once the interpreter finds that the value of the variable "y" is 5, it exits the loop completely. This explains the source of the output.

The "continue" statement

When this statement is used, the interpreter exits execution of the remaining block, and begins executing the next iteration. Consider the example shown below:

```
<script type="text/javascript">

<!--

var y = 5;

document.write("Getting into the loop<br /> ");

while (y < 20)

{

y = y + 1;

if (y == 10){

continue;  // the rest of the loop body will be skipped
```

```
    }

    document.write( y + "<br />");

    }

    document.write("Now leaving the loop!<br /> ");

    //-->

</script>
```

You can write the program, save it, and then open it with your browser. You will observe the following output:

Getting into the loop
6
7
8
9
11
12
13
14
15
16
17
18
19
20
Now leaving the loop!

Notice how we have used the "*continue*" statement to skip

printing the value of y when it is equal to 10.

Labels for controlling the flow

This involves the use of an identifier followed by a semicolon. It is usually applied to either a block of code or a single statement. Consider the example shown below:

```
<script type="text/javascript">

<!--

document.write("Getting into the loop!<br /> ");

oloop:   // Name of the label

for (var j = 1; j < 10; j++)

{

document.write("The oloop: " + j + "<br />");

iloop:

for (var k = 1; k < 10; k++)
```

```javascript
{

if (k > 4 ) break ;       // Leave the innermost loop

if (j == 3) break iloop; // perform the same act

if (j == 5) break oloop; // Leave the outer loop

document.write("The iloop: " + k + "  <br />");

}

}

document.write("Now leaving the loop!<br /> ");

//-->

</script>
```

You can write the program, save, and then open it with the browser. You should get the following output:

Getting into the loop!
The oloop: 1
The iloop: 1
The iloop: 2
The iloop: 3
The iloop: 4
The oloop: 2
The iloop: 1
The iloop: 2
The iloop: 3
The iloop: 4
The oloop: 3
The oloop: 4
The iloop: 1
The iloop: 2
The iloop: 3
The iloop: 4
The oloop: 5
Now leaving the loop!

Consider the next example shown below:

<script type="text/javascript">

<!--

**document.write("Getting into the loop!
 ");**

```
oloop:   // This is the name of the label

for (var j = 1; j< 5; j++)

{

document.write("oloop: " + j + "<br />");

for (var k = 1; k < 10; k++)

{

if (k == 5){

continue oloop;

}

document.write("iloop: " + k + "<br />");

}

}
```

```
document.write("Now leaving the loop!<br /> ");
```

```
//-->
```

```
</script>
```

Again, write the program, save, and then open it with your browser. You will get the following result:

Getting into the loop!
oloop: 1
iloop: 1
iloop: 2
iloop: 3
iloop: 4
oloop: 2
iloop: 1
iloop: 2
iloop: 3
iloop: 4
oloop: 3
iloop: 1
iloop: 2
iloop: 3
iloop: 4
oloop: 4
iloop: 1
iloop: 2
iloop: 3
iloop: 4
Now leaving the loop!

Chapter 13:

Cookies in Javascript

These are applied in commercial websites. They have the purpose of maintaining a session regarding different web pages. This is not the case with normal websites where the server and the web browser use HTTP protocol for communication. With cookies, one can monitor the activity done by a user on a website.

Cookies take the following syntax:

document.cookie =
"key1=value1;key2=value2;expires=date";

If you set the expiration date, then the cookie will definitely expire during that specified date and even time. However, this attribute is optional. Consider the example given below:

```html
<html>

<head>

<script type="text/javascript">

<!--

function CreateCookie()

{

if( document.myform.customer.value == "" ){

alert("Provide a value!");

return;

}
```

```javascript
cvalue= escape(document.myform.customer.value) +
";";

document.cookie="name=" + cvalue;

alert("Now setting the cookies : " + "name=" + cvalue
);

}

//-->

</script>

</head>

<body>

<form name="myform" action="">
```

```
Provide your name: <input type="text"
name="name"/>

<input type="button" value="Create Cookie"
onclick="CreateCookie();"/>

</form>

</body>

</html>
```

You can write the above program, save the file and then open it with your browser. The following output will be observed:

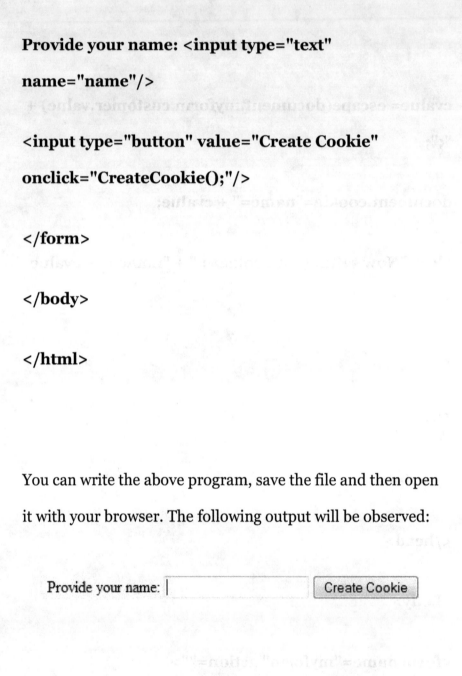

You can type in your name and then press the button written "*Create Cookie.*".This will create a cookie in your machine. To set multiple cookies, use multiple *key=value* and separate them using a comma.

Reading cookies

Consider the example given below:

```html
<html>

<head>

<script type="text/javascript">

<!--

function RCookie()

{

var acookies = document.cookie;

alert("Available cookies : " + acookies );
```

```
// Put cookies in an array in pairs

carray = acookies.split(';');



// taking the key value pairs out of the arrays.

for(var j=0; j<carray.length; j++){

nm= carray[j].split('=')[0];

val = carray[j].split('=')[1];

alert("The key is : " + nm + " with a value : " + val);

}

}

//-->

</script>
```

```
</head>

<body>

<form name="mform" action="">

<input type="button" value="Obtain Cookie"
onclick="RCookie()"/>

</form>

</body>

</html>
```

Again write the program, save it, and then open the file with
your browser. Observe the output which should be as follows:

Obtain Cookie

Click on the button, and observe what happens. The cookies set in the previous section will be displayed. If many cookies are displayed, then don't worry, as your machine might have some cookies being set up. The code displays all of them.

Setting the Expiration Date of a Cookie

It is possible for one to extend the lifetime of a cookie by setting an expiration date beyond that of the browser. A date and time need to be set for the *"expires"* attribute.

Consider the example given below:

\<html\>

\<head\>

\<script type="text/javascript"\>

\<!--

function WCookie()

{

var n = new Date();

```
n.setMonth( n.getMonth() + 2 );

cvalue = escape(document.myform.customer.value) +
";"

document.cookie="name=" + cvalue;

document.cookie = "expires=" + n.toUTCString() +
";"

alert("Now setting the cookies: " + "name=" + cvalue
);

}

//-->

</script>

</head>

<body>
```

```
<form name="mform" action="">

Provide name: <input type="text" name="nm"/>

<input type="button" value="Create Cookie"
onclick="WCookie()"/>

</form>

</body>

</html>
```

Deleting cookies

If you want anyone trying to read a cookie to get no result,
then you can delete it. To achieve this, just set the expiration
date of the cookie to a past time. This is demonstrated in the
following example:

```
<html>
```

```html
<head>

<script type="text/javascript">

<!--

function WCookie()

{

var n = new Date();

n.setMonth( n.getMonth() - 1 );

cvalue = escape(document.myform.customer.value) +
";"

document.cookie="name=" + cvalue;

document.cookie = "expires=" + n.toUTCString() +
";"
```

```
alert("Now Setting the Cookies : " + "name=" + cvalue
);

}

//-->

</script>

</head>

<body>

<form name="mform" action="">

Provide name: <input type="text" name="nm"/>

<input type="button" value="Create Cookie"
onclick="WCookie()"/>

</form>

</body>
```

</html>

Chapter 14:

Dialog Boxes

You can use Javascript to develop three different kinds of

dialog boxes. They can be used to prompt the user to provide

some information or convey some information to them.

Alert Dialog Box

These are mostly used to warn users of some of their actions.

Consider the example shown below:

<head>

<script type="text/javascript">

<!--

alert("Be Warned");

//-->

</script>

</head>

Just write the program, save it, and then open it with your browser. You will observe the following output:

As observed, the background will be blurred for emphasis to be on the warning message.

Confirmation Dialog Box

With this, a dialog box with two buttons is displayed. The two buttons are the "*Ok*" and the "*Cancel*" ones. They are intended to take the option or consent of a user. Consider the example shown below:

<head>

<script type="text/javascript">

<!--

var rVal = confirm("Are you sure that you want to delete ?");

if(rVal == true){

alert("You chose to continue!");

```
return true;

}else{

Alert("You do not want to continue!");

return false;

}

//-->

</script>

</head>
```

Once again, save the program in a file, and then open the file with a browser. Observe the output that it gives. On the dialog that will appear, click on the "*Ok*" button and observe what will happen. Click on the "*Cancel*" button, and observe the effect.

Prompt Dialog Box

With this box, the user can provide input, and then click on the "*Ok*" button. The necessary action will then be taken on the input. Write the program shown below:

```html
<head>

<script type="text/javascript">

<!--

var val = prompt("Provide your name : ", "enter name here");

alert("Your name is : " + val );

//-->

</script>

</head>
```

After writing the program, just save it as usual, and then launch it with your browser. The following will be the output:

Just provide your name in the text field as directed, and then click on the "*Ok*" button. The following result will then be observed:

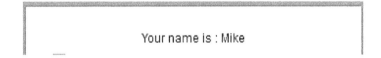

Conclusion

It can be concluded that jQuery is a Javascript library designed to make client-side scripting of HTML much easier. With jQuery, both the Javascript and the HTML are separated, whereby for one to add event handlers to the Data Object Model (DOM), Javascript must be used rather than doing it using the HTML event attributes to call Javascript functions. To use jQuery, one can do it in two ways.

The first way involves downloading the jQuery and then keeping it in the same folder as the web application you are developing. However, the path where you have stored this must be clearly specified within the header of the program. The second choice involves using it while in the Content Delivery Network (CDN), whereby you just have to specify the path where it is located. It is also possible to handle events with jQuery. This will have the effect of making the created user interface do something.

With jQuery, one can add numerous effects to their web application so as to make it amazing to the users. A set of user interfaces for a web application can also be created with jQuery.

Javascript is the most widely used language in the world today, and is well known for its simplicity of use. It is a complete programming language on its own, and it supports object oriented programming. It has a strong support for flow control where the flow of logic can be controlled. One can create numerous dialog boxes with jQuery.